Steps for Deeper Understanding

As you reflect on your life at this time in your life, what are you becoming?

Where do you need to see beyond "the obvious" to something greater or deeper?

As you meditate on this, feel the process of transformation happening from deep within you.

Notes:_____

_____

_____

_____

ATTITUDE

Studies have shown that people who have a positive attitude are healthier physically, mentally, and emotionally. They tend to heal faster from an illness or an operation. Obviously, attitude makes a great difference in the quality of life and how people live it. Much evidence suggests that even — especially — when people have to deal with very difficult situations, attitude is one of their most important choices. Why? Because we energetically draw to ourselves what we focus our attention on. I would prefer to look for the bright side of a situation as quickly as I can, rather than get caught up in misery and depression. A positive attitude can be a saving grace.

PROSPERITY

> *Prosperity is a way of living and thinking, and not just money or things. Poverty is a way of living and thinking, and not just a lack of money or things.*
>
> — *Eric Butterworth*

Universal principles are just that, universal. These principles are unchangeable. You cannot *not* use them. However, you can learn about them, and use them rightly, purposely, and consistently. And wait — there's more! The way the universe works, if you are misusing the universal principles, their results will show you just that. You get to try it again in a *new* way, or you can just keep on doing what you have always done and getting the same results. How you use the principles is up to you.

DAY 13: IT'S THE LAW

What keeps us from being all we are created to be? What keeps us from making the positive difference in this world that we can make if we share our gifts, our talents, and our innate abilities a little more? What do we fear losing if we give? The great law of the universe, a very provable law, is that *as we give, so do we receive.* Most of us know this, yet we often forget that the law *is* the law. We don't change the law. The only choice we have, really, is to understand and apply universal principles in our lives, or to ignore principles and wonder why things work out the way they do.

Some people consider themselves spiritual people. They follow the rituals, rules, and regulations they have been brought up to follow. Yet, sometimes, life situations simply do not work out the way these people hoped for. I have never met anyone whose life has happened exactly as expected. Whether you have had a strict religious upbringing, an eclectic religious experience, or even none at all, you have certain expectations of life. In addition, those expectations change over time as you change.

Being spiritual is not about whether you go to a church or temple, how many times you go, or how much dedication or fervor you demonstrate. Each person is spiritual. Nobody is anything but a spiritual person. As Pierre Teilhard de Chardin said so many years ago, "We are not human beings having a spiritual experience; *we are spiritual beings having a human experience.*" Spirituality, like so many other aspects of life, is not about what *is*, but about *awakening* to what is.

Mark Twain once remarked, "When I was a boy of 14, my father was so ignorant I could hardly stand to have the old man around. But when I got to be 21, I was astonished at how much the old man had learned in seven years."

We also have much to learn. We can grow as individuals and as communities in ways that help us understand and support one another. We can be the answer to one another's difficulties or questions. How beautiful it would be if we approached life, and each other, as opportunities to learn, grow, and serve, rather than as competitions.

The other day, I was in my car. Someone was coming my way, coming "out" the "in" driveway. I saw the shock, and then the instant remorse, in the driver's eyes as he realized his error. I waited the few seconds for him to back up and re-route his car. However, the driver behind me could not understand that a few moments of kindness, patience, and understanding was in order. That driver laid on his car horn, yelling and gesturing as he swung rapidly around me.

I would like to say that I took that in as would a saint, but I did not. I waved back (although not rudely) and let the man have his anger. Yet, for a moment, I felt righteously indignant, justifying my position (the entire episode took only ten seconds, after all) and not necessarily wishing the best and holiest of consequences on this ignorant honker. But suddenly I realized we are all in times of stress, at least occasionally. I shifted my energy, sending this upset driver thoughts of peace and prayers that he would be able to release the stress and anger that caused him to react so rashly to such a small delay.

Instantly, I felt peace where I had felt tension. I felt openness where I had felt defensiveness. I realized the simplicity of the law I teach, the universal principle, and the application of this principle. None of us are able to escape universal law. *As we give, so do we receive.*

We each have so much to give: our talents, our experience, and our willingness to help others live a more fulfilling life. What do we fear losing by giving? If we just take a moment to reflect, we know that our greatest joy, our highest sense of creativity, our most transformative times have come from sharing with others the essence of who we are. The soul grows as we give, an acknowledgement of the value we see in another person as well as the value we see in ourselves. In truth, this giving is an acknowledgement of our realization and acceptance of the activity of Spirit in us, of God in us as spiritual beings, having a human experience.

Steps for Deeper Understanding

Think back on your spiritual teachings over time. Name one or two that you see much differently than you did as a child.

If you knew, without a doubt, that a thought, prayer, or action from you today would grow and return to you at some future time, what would you think, pray, or do?

Take a few minutes to go within and connect with the spiritual truth that you are much more than a physical being. Awaken to your higher self!

Notes:_____

_____

_____

_____

DAY 14: TO TELL THE TRUTH

I searched for years for the Truth. That's like the "truth," but with a capital "T" — not just _my_ truth, but _the_ Truth. Many people will be more than happy to tell you the truth as they see it, but that truth is always subjective, always tainted in some way by a person's experience.

I had heard enough of other people's perceptions. As interesting as those viewpoints might be, I wanted to know what was absolute, what was unchangeable, what I could count on in life. Certain universal truths are not tied to one religion but are found in all religions in some form. Those are the Truths I yearned to find.

I was seeking information that was more spiritual than religious. Religion is really nothing more than spiritual formatting, a way to apply what goes beyond our everyday reason into a way of living for the followers of that religion.

Most religions believe in the importance of loving one another. Specific guidelines with certain rules and regulations have been established over time, but love is the basis of most, if not all, religions.

Religion also supposes the existence of a higher power above and beyond mortal existence. Some groups see this power as far distant, and others see it as immanent, inherent. The acceptance of a higher power helps support a mystical perspective to existence, as opposed to a theory that can be calculated in the same way mathematics can be.

Another shared basic Truth (although stated in various forms) affirms that what we put out into the world comes back to us. What goes around comes around, the saying goes. To me, this great Truth can be easily proven in our lives. In Unity, we call it the Law of Mind Action, understanding that "thoughts held in mind produce after their own kind."

If I am holding on to fearful or resentful thoughts about a relationship, for instance, I am building more fear or resentment in my own life. How can I continually find things to complain about and then feel any true sense of happiness? I create by the thoughts I think and the feelings I hold on to. "As you give, so do you receive" is a familiar saying; however, this Truth has little to do with *what* you give, but *how* you give. Giving my financial gift to my spiritual center with appreciation and joy makes a statement to the universe that places abundance of all good things into the equation. I can know that as I give (with appreciation and joy), so shall I receive.

Prove to yourself that the energy you project returns to you multiplied. Give lovingly and lavishly. This energy is one of the secrets to prosperity, which encompasses happiness, wholeness, and a sense of purpose in life.

A person once commented to me, "Rev. Dan, you say that what I think about grows, and all I have been thinking about lately is money. But it's not growing, it's diminishing!" After some investigation and discussion, I realized that this person was not really thinking about money, but *lack of it*, and the great Law was certainly proving itself! Think about and feel lack, and you create more of it. Conversely, when you consider the many ways you have been blessed, the opportunities you have been afforded, as well as the relationships you have had and from which you have learned so much about yourself and about life, you emit a different energy. When you decide to give rather than receive, counterintuitively, you receive in greater ways.

Other universal Truths deserve to be shared at another time. However, this Law of Mind Action bears proving in each person's life as the key to happiness, the opportunity to alleviate suffering, and the way to truly, positively transform every life. As you believe, so it is for you — and as it goes around, it comes around!

Steps for Deeper Understanding

Observe your feelings when you give someone a compliment or provide them needed help.

Notice your feelings when you voluntarily give money to a person or an organization, remembering that how you give and not what you give makes the greatest difference. Begin to notice how your energy comes back to you in unexpected ways.

Are you "stuck" in an area of your life? In what ways can you re-frame your relation to this area and open up to more positive possibilities?

Notes:_____

_____

_____

_____

GRATITUDE

*The miracle of gratitude is that it shifts your perception
to such an extent that it changes the world you see.*

— Dr. Robert Holden

What good does it do to express gratitude? We may seem beholden to someone or something if we show thanks or appreciation. We got to where we are pretty much by ourselves, didn't we? Nobody else sat through endless hours of schooling and training to learn what we eventually learned, did they? Nope. Nobody else got up in the morning to go off to work for us. No way. We did it ourselves, all the way.

— *These thoughts have been brought to you by poverty consciousness.* —

In truth, gratitude is a beautiful force that brings much good into our lives. Parts of this chapter refer to a specific celebration of gratitude; however, we can observe thanksgiving every day.

DAY 15: ARE YOU GRATEFUL ENOUGH?

I am so grateful for so much. But I am not grateful enough.

It's true. When I get in my car to go to work or run an errand, I do not generally consider the incredible benefit that having a car brings me. I do not always consciously appreciate that when it's hot outside, my car cools me down. I do not generally acknowledge that I have roads to take me wherever I want to go. And on and on it goes. I believe most of us take so much for granted in our day-to-day lives. We have food to eat, food to spare, and even food to share. We have a place to be, and we have people who care about us.

Now, sometimes we may feel particularly grateful. We may have narrowly escaped what could have been a tragic car accident, for example. After our hearts calm down, we consider how lucky we were and may even go so far as to utter a brief prayer of gratitude. But those instances are the exceptions, not the norm.

Have you ever received those emails trying to make you feel good about yourself by comparing your situation to that of someone else? You might read something like "The next time you feel like complaining about how far you had to walk, consider the person who was in an accident and cannot walk at all" or "The next time you feel like grumbling about how your steak is overcooked, consider the poor people who have not eaten in three days."

I really detest those emails. While the sender probably wants us to change our perspective of life, which *does* have merit, this method can also result in an *increase* of comparing ourselves to others. If we do that, we will always be considering ourselves better or worse than others, a false premise.

Certainly, many people need food and other necessities. But my awareness of that situation would be better directed toward helping those people get whatever they need. In addition, by comparing myself to other people, I begin making many assumptions about them. I can never truly know another person's whole story.

What I do know is that we will all have to face uncertainty from time to time. We may have vibrant health one day and find ourselves dealing with a difficult illness or accident another day.

What we have is *this* day. This day is the now into which we pour our emotions, actions, and thoughts. This day is one in which we can look for and find much to be grateful for, no matter what our conditions are. Although we can find what isn't working and put our attention on feeling bad about that, we can find what isn't working and *do what we can to make it work better.*

Even when we face difficulties, we can expect some good to come out of them. We can remember that within every adversity is a seed of positive possibilities.

Charles Fillmore, co-founder of the Unity movement, explained, "Gratitude is a great mind magnet, and when it is expressed from the spiritual standpoint it is powerfully augmented. The saying of grace at the table has its origin in this idea of the power of increase through giving thanks."

Gratitude is a magnet that draws to us more to be grateful for. As we move through this day, let's at least give this idea a try. Take a moment to breathe in deeply and consider what is blessing you today: your health, your friends, your family, your belongings, your ability to live in this beautiful world.

We can feel immense gratitude for much that we have today. That gratitude will draw to us even more to be thankful for.

Steps for Deeper Understanding

List five things for which you have gratitude right now.

Practice beginning and ending each day with thoughts of gratitude.

The next time a complaint comes to mind, stop, breathe, and be thankful for your blessings instead.

Notes:_____

_____

_____

_____

DAY 16: THANKS IN ALL THINGS

I once read about a missionary to Africa who was working with many tribes in the area. One of the tribes had to deal with poverty much more than the others nearby. Wondering what the cause could be, the missionary made a startling discovery: that tribe had no words to express thanks. He wondered about a possible connection with their ongoing poverty.

Giving thanks opens a door of giving and receiving. If the door is locked shut, no back-and-forth flow can occur.

In the *2003 Journal of Personality and Social Psychology*, Dr. Robert A. Emmons of the University of California, Davis and Dr. Michael E. McCullough of the University of Miami shared a study, "Counting Blessings Versus Burdens: An Experimental Investigation of Gratitude and Subjective Well-Being in Daily Life."

Their initial scientific study indicates that gratitude plays a significant role in a person's sense of well-being. In the study, groups of people tracked events in their lives. One group included all daily events. A second group tracked only their unpleasant experiences each day. The third group compiled a list of things for which they felt gratitude each day.

Not surprisingly, the gratitude group received many benefits: greater levels of enthusiasm and energy, more exercise, better sleep, and less overall stress in their lives. This group felt "on purpose" with their lives.

Our church congregation received "gratitude journals" to track daily a few things for which they felt thankful. The journal included a card suggesting steps to make gratitude a daily habit.

I have a friend in Texas who makes these gratitude journals and cards available to his followers. He says it has been incredible and life-changing for him, as well, to see how a re-focus of attention can cause such a difference in lives. Too often we all get caught up in our daily busyness, or even drift into fault-finding and complaint.

However, a daily practice of looking for and finding the good already in our lives seems to draw more to us to be thankful for!

Feeling thankful naturally leads us to express our thanks in many ways. We appreciate life and live to our fullest potential. We give to others. We give to causes. We give back to where we have felt especially blessed. Gratitude is a wonderful feeling, but extending that gratitude to others, giving of ourselves, is an even greater feeling! According to William Arthur Ward, "Feeling gratitude and not expressing it is like wrapping a present and not giving it away."

As I write this, I am deep in the season of gratitude. Thanksgiving is around the corner. With all the gatherings and the holiday hubbub, taking some time in quiet reminiscence to consider how many people have touched us in ways that have made positive impacts is appropriate and important.

We give thanks for food and shelter, for loved ones, for a sense of belonging and purpose on this beautiful planet. We look for and find ways to share the good that has come to us. We especially thank God, by whatever name, for giving us the opportunity to be a conduit of the flow of infinite good back into the world. We give thanks in all things!

Steps for Deeper Understanding

Spend a few minutes in meditation. Relax. Breathe in deeply.

Envision someone in your life you truly appreciate.

In this meditation time, notice at least five reasons you appreciate this person. Sit in the moment, feeling the fullness of your appreciation.

Notes:_____

_____

_____

_____

OPEN TO MIRACLES

"There are only two ways to live your life. One is as though nothing is a miracle. The other is as though everything is a miracle."

— *Albert Einstein*

I am open to miracles! I believe miracles as everyday occurrences. We are normally just blind to miracles, unless we decide to notice. Noticing miracles is a decision that, when made regularly, becomes a way of life. I never tire of miracles, and I love seeing people's reactions to them — the amazing healing, the fortuitous coincidence, the divine idea that is a solution to what had seemed an impossible situation. The more we look for and expect miracles, the more they appear. (Surprise — they've been there all along!)

DAY 17: NEXT STEPS

I consider myself to be one of the luckiest people in the world. I get to share in the joys of others as they share the miracles that happen in their lives: getting married or christening a child, for example. I also get to share with others as they face difficulties, seemingly impossible situations, and losses: of jobs, marriages, vibrant health, or loved ones by death.

I get to experience with others these highs and lows of life, holding to a constant faith that, although things do indeed sometimes look bleak, or even hopeless, we can make it through and come out the other end stronger.

Not only do I believe in miracles, but I also believe no one miracle is really greater than any other. Miracles just take different forms. I've also learned over time that one's attitude can make a major difference in the appearance of miracles.

Quantum physics states that we actually affect what we observe *by the act of observing*! By extension, I postulate that we have an effect on the *conditions* of our lives by how we choose to see them.

This does not mean we should ignore the obvious. When we break a leg, we break a leg. A broken leg is painful, inconvenient, and may even limit us for a time, but the condition does not have to define us. Similarly, we can choose how we see anything that comes our way: the ups and downs, the obstacles, and the successes. By observing, by opening to the unlimited possibilities of Spirit, of the universe, we usher in the miracles.

You have likely experienced miracles. Have you found something that you were sure was lost? Have you had an unexplainable coincidence bring a helpful person into your life? Have you had a physical or emotional healing?

I know a man who was facing many depressing obstacles. He had recently become divorced. His job security was uncertain, like many other coworkers' jobs.

Somehow, though, he remained hopeful that these problems would work out, even if that outcome seemed far from possible. He heard about a workshop to help people gain a new perspective about life and decided to attend and take his mind off his problems. This uplifting experience re-charged him about being open to positive possibilities in his life.

He couldn't explain why, but he just felt better. His boss did indeed call him into the office. But instead of being fired, he was offered a $10,000 raise because of his diligence and commitment to the job. Although the business had to cut back in some areas and lay off some people, management did not want to lose those most important to the success of the business, and they saw value in him.

I need to remind myself from time to time (and I will offer to you) that we are more than just physical beings suffering our way through life. As Ernest Holmes declared, "We are spiritual beings, living in a spiritual universe, governed by spiritual law." Our existence includes a force that is greater than our circumstances, and yet accessible to us through the power of our thoughts, words, and feelings.

I am no longer surprised by miracles — I am simply delighted! Miracles are happening all the time. Our part in miracles is simply to be open to them. We can choose how we think, speak and even feel about our life circumstances. When we put our attention on the positive possibilities, regardless of the limiting appearances, we affect the outcome. And in many ways, that ability makes each one of us the luckiest person in the world.

Steps for Deeper Understanding

Think about the words you use to describe your life when someone asks how you are doing.

Certain words or phrases you may use to describe yourself or your life can limit you. List some specific examples of limiting words or phrases you may have used.

Affirm the positive today. Choose your words as though you are creating a new life for yourself, and know that, indeed, you are!

Notes:_____

_____

_____

_____

DAY 18: IMAGINE A MIRACULOUS DAY/YEAR/LIFE

We look at a new year with hopes of new beginnings; however, every day must be made new. How do you want your day, your year, your life to be? What if you could do anything you wanted, go anywhere you wanted, accomplish anything you wanted? Do you have any idea where you would begin? Do you know what you really want? I believe we can accomplish much more by making simple, yet powerful changes to our limited thinking.

I believe that each day is filled with infinite possibilities for good. What can we do to help bring these good possibilities into manifestation? Just as importantly, what might we do to accidentally keep our good from us?

Our ability to think allows us to use our power of imagination. Used incorrectly, our imagination can exaggerate negative possibilities. Used correctly, our imagination allows us to envision the positive possibilities. A good New Year (or any "new day") resolution is to notice the thoughts we think and the words we use to express those thoughts.

We always have a choice. We can be critical, cynical, and anxious, finding evidence that supports negative or dismal thoughts and feelings; or, we can change our thoughts and words to reflect a positive expectation. All circumstances have at least the seed of a positive outcome, change, or possibility, even if that is learning what *not* to do.

I + F = R [Imagination plus Faith equals Results] is a formula that works. Albert Einstein considered imagination to be more important than knowledge. We want to use our imagination, combined with the power of faith, in productive, creative ways that point us in the direction of our greatest desires.

Too often, though, we seek the negative. Here's a scenario demonstrating misuse of imagination. A woman comes home from having lunch with a friend at a new restaurant in town. Later, she opens her purse to review the receipt and finds that her wallet is missing. "Oh no!" she thinks. "I must have left it at the restaurant. Now it's probably been stolen. That waiter looked kind of shady anyway. And I had $180 in cash. Oh, no! My credit cards are in there, too. He's probably racking up thousands of dollars in debt on my account. I'll never be able to pay that back. Oh, no! He's ruining my credit, too. And now he's even got my personal information from my driver's license, and he'll steal my identity and everything I have! Oh, no! If he has my driver's license, then he has my address. I'll never be safe in my own home! I'll have to move! But wait — what's that on the dresser? Oh! My wallet..."

Worry is a misuse of the imagination, combining with faith in a most negative way. Would you rather be right about something terrible you imagined, or would you rather be in the flow of a positive way of life?

I'm still open for miracles for everyone. I believe that we can open the door to infinite, positive possibilities by thinking enlightened thoughts.

As attributed to Deepak Chopra in *Synchrodestiny*, "According to Vedanta, there are only two symptoms of enlightenment, just two indications that a transformation is taking place within you toward a higher consciousness. The first symptom is that you stop worrying. Things don't bother you anymore. You become light-hearted and full of joy. The second symptom is that you encounter more and more meaningful coincidences in your life, more and more synchronicities. And this accelerates to the point where you actually experience the miraculous."

I am making some fairly specific plans for my life, and I am also open to the many miracles that may occur. I hope and pray that you, too, are open in mind and heart to all the good you can possibly receive. Imagine that!

Steps for Deeper Understanding

Imagine, without time or financial constraints, some area of your life you want to enrich.

Notice any resistance you have in believing it is possible to make this enrichment a reality.

Open to guidance by asking, "What are my next steps as I venture forward in faith?"

Notes:_____

_____

_____

_____

DAY 19: DO YOU WANT FRIES WITH THAT?

Are your conversations with God two-sided? Or do you find yourself generally doing all the talking, telling the Supreme Universal Being, creator of all things, what isn't working in your life and expecting changes? Sometimes people think of God (by whatever name) as the great drive-thru in the sky. We pull up to give our order, swing around the corner, and expect our exact order to be there — super-sized, if possible. When our order doesn't look like our request, we blame the establishment, or at least the order-taker.

But what if what we received was exactly what was best for us at the time? Could it ever be that when our desperate prayers are unanswered, a higher prayer is being answered? Often, we don't get our way; but later, looking back, we realize that by getting our way, we would have missed out on a greater good. I call that "blessings in disguise."

What if we ordered the wrong thing? You might think, "I'm sure I asked for the perfect man or woman in my life, but somehow I got another one just like before! What happened?" Or you might note, "I ordered my perfect job and thought I received it. Instead, I got another irrational and demanding boss again!"

Of course, we are the cause of the chaos. The good news is that we can decide to take responsibility for our lives and behave differently.

Although we are clearly able to assert our will in life and make things happen, perhaps we can open ourselves more to direction, guidance, and enlightenment. If we listen and truly hear the voice or influence of Spirit, if we exercise patience, if we are willing to receive alternative ideas, we find peace and purpose.

Dan, a man I know, once bought a house to rescue his failing marriage. The bank turned down the loan (a clue from the universe), but he persevered. Dan gathered evidence to prove that the bank *had* to grant his request. Eventually, the bank came around. Dan became the proud homeowner of a home he could not afford — and his marriage ended anyway.

Why didn't he listen? Dan later admitted that buying the house never really felt right, that he just wanted to impose his somewhat frantic will on life because he felt out of control. Dan had pulled up to the Divine Drive-Thru, requested and picked up his order, but only later realized he ordered the wrong thing. Deeper understanding of healthy relationships might have been a better request, but that choice would have required that Dan be still and listen for a few moments.

(By the way, I know this man because I am this man.)

Our conversations with God are best if they are two-sided. We ask; then we listen. We can learn to trust our gut feeling, our intuitive nature. Generally, the answers we seek are closer than we think. When we get out of the way, the way is made clear. Life's not a Divine Drive-Thru, but it is food for thought.

Steps for Deeper Understanding

Look back over your life and notice one or two situations you thought were "bad" at the time, but now see were blessings in disguise.

Are there any areas of your life today in which you find yourself being "willful" (for all the right reasons, of course!)?

Bring any willfulness into a conversation with God, speak your mind, and then LISTEN.

Notes:_____

_____

_____

_____

LOVE

"The best and most beautiful things in this world cannot be seen or even heard but must be felt with the heart."

— *Helen Keller*

Nothing is as strong as the universal harmonizer, love. Why do we resist? Why are we afraid of sharing our love? Maybe we remember a hurt, a heartbreak based on unmet expectations. Maybe we fear our love will be misused somehow. Nevertheless, love is generally the answer to our best approach to life, and the rewards are many for those who have the courage to express that love.

DAY 20: THE POWER OF LOVE

A young lady who had never met her grandfather was looking at some old photographs with her grandmother. The girl knew that her grandmother was taller than her grandfather but didn't realize how much until she saw the photos. When the granddaughter asked how tall they both were, her grandmother replied that she was 5' 11" and he had been 5' 6."

"Grandma," the girl blurted out, "how could you have fallen in love with a man who was so much shorter than you?"

"Honey," her grandmother replied, "we fell in love sitting down, and by the time we stood up, it was just too late."

Love has the power to overcome seeming obstacles in life. Love brings aid to those in need in the form of compassion and healing to the soul in the form of acceptance without judgment. Luckily for all of us, love is not a commodity, but an innate power we all have. We can give love freely and never run out. As a matter of fact, love seems to have an inverse mathematical relationship, multiplying the more we give it away!

I sometimes wonder why some folks are so protective of the love they give. Perhaps they have never learned how to freely give of themselves or have not been shown much love by others. Some people have been (or think they have been) hurt by love. They may have given love to others and not received love in kind. In truth, they are not hurt by love, but by their expectations of others. Giving to *get* rarely works out the way a person expects. For these people, perhaps love in the form of forgiveness is the place to start. Forgiving is really an act of self-love. By forgiving —letting go of your resentment — you release that other person from holding power over you. Forgiving is part of the healing process.

Starting, or growing, the experience of love is easy, considering the innumerable opportunities to do so: a smile or a kind word to the cashier at the grocery store or to a neighbor or co-worker, for example.

Love is more than an emotion. To expand the growth of this power you may decide to extend a gesture of thoughtfulness to another person or to a cause in the form of service. I have found at my church that people who give of themselves in service report that they receive much more than they give. Giving of ourselves also helps us feel better about who we are and helps us develop meaning and purpose in our lives. As people feel valuable and valued, they can learn to love themselves for who they are, for their uniqueness, and for the vital part they play in the lives of others.

Of course, one of the primary ways we share love is with our family, especially with our "significant others." One of the most powerful and sacred commitments we can make is to promise our love to another person as a life partner. I have had the good fortune to officiate hundreds of weddings and holy unions over the last quarter century. These commitments have taken place in churches, chapels, clubhouses, golf courses, hotels, parks, beaches, and homes. When two people face each other before witnesses to verbally share their desire to make their coupleship official, they create a holy moment. Whether the couple is young or older, with or without children, neophytes or pros in the ways of the world, their vulnerability holds astonishing power in that moment.

Often, around Valentine's Day, our church invites couples to reaffirm their commitment to each other in the form of a Renewal of Vows, or a Recommitment Ceremony. With eyes and hearts filled with love, couples once again publicly declare their love for each other in this beautiful ceremony.

Whether you are in a relationship or not, whether you are "feelin' the love" or not, I invite you to take time to consider all the love you have received and to allow the power of love to grow within you. You can open to the divine experience that love brings. When you decide to express love in its many forms more regularly, you will, indeed, feel love in return.

Steps for Deeper Understanding

Look for ways to show kindness today as an act of love —a smile, a kind word— and notice how you feel.

Investigate volunteer opportunities you can try. Start small if you wish. Notice how you feel.

Think about someone you love. Make a list, either in your mind or on paper, of the many ways you appreciate that person. Notice how you feel.

Notes:_____

_____

_____

_____

DAY 21: LOVE IS THE ANSWER

On Valentine's Day we find ways to demonstrate the love we feel for those we care for in our lives. This day has changed over time. Past typical activities included sending flowers, buying boxes of candy, shopping for the perfect card to express our feelings, gifting the love of our life with the perfect jewelry, and reserving a table at a posh restaurant. Some persons proposed marriage on this day, while others actually got married on Valentine's Day.

Nowadays, people still buy holiday flowers but usually at the local grocery store rather than delivered by a florist. Popular Valentine candy may now be dark chocolate, sugar-free, or gluten-free, or some combination of these. The card may be sent electronically from Hallmark, American Greetings, or Blue Mountain online. The popularity of jewelry or an expensive dinner at a fine restaurant as top celebration choices is waning. We are in a hurry, prizing convenience more than ever before. Maybe it's time to re-evaluate our priorities and re-identify what has true meaning in our lives. After all, we can demonstrate our love for another person in an infinite number of ways.

One of the deepest demonstrations of love is offering our presence. Even more than presents, being with and truly listening to another person with kindness and patience is a gift that makes a difference in another's heart. In our busy world, too little credit is given to the loving gift of time spent with another. When we look back at the meaningful times in our lives, we remember our feelings more than the physical gifts we received. Hallmark Cards found success with the slogan, "When you care enough to send the very best." Even if you keep the cards (I'm a softy, and I do), you remember the feeling, not the card.

Love is a power that heals, a power that uplifts. Love is the great harmonizing force in the universe. Emmett Fox, a renowned metaphysician, wrote: "Love is by far the most important thing of all. . . . There is no difficulty that enough love will not conquer. . . .

It makes no difference in your life how deeply seated may be the trouble. How hopeless the outlook. How muddled the tangle. How great the mistake. A sufficient realization of love will dissolve it all. If only you could love enough, you would be the happiest and most powerful being in all the world."

Jesus expressed the power of love this way: "I give you a new commandment, that you love one another. Just as I have loved you, you also should love one another." John 13:34 (NRSV)

So often, however, people look at love backward. They are looking for ways to receive love rather than ways to show or to give love. I have heard people say, "I have so much love to give, if only I could find someone to give it to." So they keep themselves from expressing love in other ways, waiting for Mr. or Ms. Right. They hold on to their "love energy" feeling empty and unfulfilled. Maybe they have been hurt before, but what a price to pay!

I have also seen people who easily demonstrate love for all people they come in contact with, from a special kindness shown to the grocery clerk to a smile offered to a stranger. These people draw love to themselves. They come from an attitude of love, from a place of positive expectations, and from a purposeful choice to love. With their caring and accepting actions, they uplift others.

What a difference we would make in each other's lives and in our own if we chose to express the love that is innately ours! Kindness costs nothing. Compassion is a gift that blesses the giver and the receiver. If we want more love in our lives, then we must create more. Let us make a conscious choice to express love to those already close to us, in ways we will both fondly remember. Let us demonstrate patience, acceptance, and understanding to all we meet. Let us not miss a chance to love one another. It's time.

Steps for Deeper Understanding

To whom can you show more loving attention today? How will you do that?

Are you withholding your love from anyone? If so, can you see how you are keeping love from yourself, as well?

What is one thing you can do today to show you feel valued and valuable to yourself?

Notes:_____

_____

_____

DAY 22: GOD'S LOVE IN THE FORM OF GRACE

Do you feel an element of grace in your life? Grace is here for each of us, if we keep our eyes and ears (and heart) open. Too many of us, though, may not feel like we deserve to get a break in life. Or we are spending too much time comparing ourselves to others, who *always* seem to get the breaks. Grace comes to us from unexpected sources, at unexpected times, and in unexpected ways. Grace may show up as the perfect idea at the perfect time, a forgiveness, or a way forward when none seemed apparent. We may receive guidance of some sort, or an ability to change our perspective, or a serendipitous event.

In *Celebrate Yourself*, minister and author Eric Butterworth wrote, "It is true that 'as you sow so do you reap.' Yet, God's desire to express completely through you and as you is so great that you never completely reap the harvest of error, and you always reap more good than you sow. This is grace."

At the core of grace is an inner realization that we are always one with God and that the only separation is in our mind. Grace is available to all of us, not to just a chosen few. I have heard (and in the past even said) the expression "There but for the grace of God go you or I." Is that grace? To see someone walking down the street carrying a bag or pushing a cart with all their worldly belongings and then compare that to your good fortune is not grace. But it could be. Let me explain.

We are in this world together. All of us. Perhaps seeing someone in need is an opportunity for you to be the grace of God in *their* life. If you are not guided to help someone directly, at least hold a prayerful thought for that person, or, even better, donate to an organization that is designed to help those situations.

I believe that although we cannot call upon and demand grace, we can be open to it. I also believe we sometimes block or hinder grace, a form of God's love, from our lives. When we engage in negative thinking, seeing only the worst in a given situation, we slow down the experience of grace. When we judge by appearance, we may be doing the same. We never really know the full story of another person's circumstances. When we spend too much time in worry and in "what if's," we keep grace at bay. Ingratitude also diminishes our ability to see, feel, and experience grace. Comparing ourselves to others does not help. Count your blessings, to be sure, but don't compare totals!

Grace can show up in the smallest of ways and yet make a great difference. In the late 1800's, Alexander III, Tsar of Russia, repressed many, especially the Jewish people. His wife Maria, though, was known for her soft and caring heart. Alexander once wrote an order to put a prisoner in exile for life. The order read, "Pardon impossible, to be sent to Siberia." Maria ostensibly saved that prisoner by simply moving the comma in the order, which then stated, "Pardon, impossible to be sent to Siberia." The prisoner went free.

We can increase our awareness of grace in our lives by staying open to all the possibilities, by holding faith, and by believing in workable outcomes. We don't need to fine-tune all the details. We can't, anyway.

My wife Kathy once needed a gall bladder operation. We had no insurance. We called several surgeons and hospitals, hoping for a gall-bladder-removal sale of some sort. The average price in Houston at the time was $16,000 to $25,000. We couldn't afford that, but we knew Kathy needed the operation. Finally, I came across a Doctor Paul James in the phone directory. I thought his two "Biblical" names might work in our favor.

We made an appointment to see Dr. James and explained our situation. To our surprise, he was affiliated with a teaching hospital and had taught this operation to interns hundreds of times. One intern in particular was just about to finish his residency and become a full surgeon. Dr. James explained that although he would be present in the operating room, this intern would perform the surgery, if we would agree to this arrangement. Seeing few options, we said yes. After stepping out and making a phone call, Dr. James returned to the room to discuss the cost.

Kathy and I each took a deep breath. We both trusted that if we had to pay the operation cost all back over the coming years, we could do so. Dr. James then handed us a form. "Please fill this out and provide a $25 check for processing. That's all you need to do. The operation and hospital stay are covered."

Amazing grace! This divine love is ours and does not depend on us earning it. Grace is a gift from God. Simply open your eyes, open your mind, and open your heart to accept the love of God in all its forms!

Steps for Deeper Understanding

Begin the day by choosing to love yourself. What will you do today to prove you are worthy of self-love?

Share a kind word or deed today with someone who does not expect it. Don't have any expectations yourself, just give. How do you feel?

Take a few moments in the quiet to feel the love and grace of God, of the Universe. Know with certainty that your higher power wants the absolute best for you. Accept it!

Notes:_____

_____

_____

_____

PRAYER/GUIDANCE

Looking behind I am filled with gratitude. Looking forward I am filled with vision. Looking upwards I am filled with strength. Looking within I discover peace.

— *Quero, Apache Prayer*

What if we are always in prayer? What if our prayers are always being answered? Whether a memorized set of words or our repeated thoughts, a prayer becomes a prayer through the feeling and faith behind it. Our opportunity is to ask, believe, and then be open to receive. I have let go of mechanically reciting prayers that I memorized but never really felt. Instead, I chose to pray with clarity, faith, and imagination while envisioning answered prayer. I have also learned (sometimes the hard way) to become aware of how I have sabotaged my prayer through error thinking. The first step toward realization is observation. Become aware of what you are thinking and feeling. These combined actions produce the energy of prayer.

DAY 23: RSVP RESPOND TO SPIRIT'S VOICE, PLEASE!

We all pray. We do. Any clear thought, especially connected to a feeling, qualifies as a prayer. When we pray, we put forth an energy that will return to us. As I was growing up, I learned various prayers for various times and circumstances: prayers before meals, different prayers at bedtime, and still others when I went to church. These prayers were not made up on the spot; rather, they were memorized and recited at the right time.

But now when I pray, I do not generally use those childhood prayers. More often than not, I pray by first developing a feeling. I imagine that my prayer is already answered, and I actually experience the feeling of my prayer being heard and responded to in the best way I can envision. I pray that way for myself and often also for others. I see them receiving whatever they need to have their prayer answered. I imagine them telling me about it: "You won't believe it, but after we prayed, I got a call the next day, and the challenge was completely resolved!"

Mark 11:24 (NRSV) reveals the simple, straightforward truth: "So I tell you, whatever you ask for in prayer, believe that you have received it, and it will be yours." Believe you *have* received it. Not believe you *will* receive it. When you pray that you *will* receive it, you put the energy and the action somewhere in the future. When you accept prayer as already answered, though, you can generate the feeling of the result with your imagination. Prayer — as a thought connected to a feeling — has great power.

Then comes the tricky part. We need to be open to receive the answer to prayer. Often, the answer comes through guidance. We are inwardly directed to perhaps take some kind of action. Maybe we need to make a phone call or start doing something we find challenging. Answered prayer does not always show up as a package from Amazon. It may come to us in ways we surmise as an inner knowing. Guidance, though, can be uncertain. How do I know it's spiritual guidance, and not my busy mind? After all, when I pray about a major concern, my mind may take a thousand turns as I consider all the possibilities.

Spiritual guidance, however, tends to come with a certain "rightness" to it, in my experience. This guidance is neither defensive nor offensive. It certainly is not always the easiest possible answer. Spiritual guidance may show up as a feeling, a coincidence, an impulse, or an inner nudge. Someone once called this guidance "the shove of the Dove." When we receive guidance, following it is up to us. That choice allows us to grow in our ability to recognize guidance more easily. We need to learn to discern. Discern comes from words that mean "to separate apart." We need to spiritually discern, to separate the inner direction (our help from God) from the mental busy-ness that runs through our brains. This practice takes not only awareness, but also courage. Yes, we may make a mistake — but we will learn to discern.

When you receive an invitation to a wedding or a party, you may also be asked to RSVP, an acronym for *Repondez s'il vous plait*, i.e., "Please respond." We recognize guidance better by following through on its invitation. This RSVP may more aptly mean "Respond to Spirit's Voice, Please." When we take the time to slow down, open up, and listen, we become aware of the guidance — often an answer to prayer — coming our way. We grow our spiritual muscles.

Instead of living in the land of procrastination or fear of making a mistake, take the giant leap to act. Slow down, open up, and listen. Then, move forward with what I call 3D Faith: Discern, Decide, and Do It! Hear the voice of God and feel the feeling that tells you what steps are yours to take next. Move forward in faith. The Reverend Doctor Martin Luther King, Jr. said, "Faith is taking the first step even when you can't see the whole staircase."

Listen. Discern, Decide, and Do It. When Spirit calls, RSVP. Respond to Spirit's Voice, Please!

Steps for Deeper Understanding

Begin to notice the nudges, feelings, and coincidences that may signal answered prayer.

Take time in the silence to discern what guidance generally feels like for you.

Take action as guided. Feel the power of following through on your spiritual guidance as you strengthen your awareness of God in you.

Notes:_____

_____

_____

_____

DAY 24: ASK THE RIGHT QUESTION

The flu season affects many people. We place hand sanitizer throughout the church to help keep viruses from spreading quite so easily. I was hit with flu once (although not as badly as others were); however, I certainly was not as ill as I had been on one memorable occasion in the past.

I learned one of my greatest lessons from that painful time.

Early in my ministerial career, I was working in a large church as the senior associate minister. Of the four Sunday services, I spoke regularly at the 12:45 p.m. service. Generally, the folks coming to that service had either been up all night or had just finished an early lunch. My opportunity was to keep them awake while I gained inspired, invaluable training.

Evidently, my senior minister had developed faith in my ability (or perhaps couldn't find a substitute on short notice). I would conduct all four Sunday services while he was out of town. My task was both a great honor and an awesome responsibility. I needed to prove I was worthy of such trust! I prepared the Sunday lesson and then practiced and practiced so I would not disappoint either the senior minister or any of those attending the services that Sunday. I had no idea how much my situation could change in just a few hours.

I declared myself ready. I had prepared the best I could, but I did not see *this* coming — *food poisoning*! Late Saturday night into Sunday morning I became so sick, in such pain, that the great questions of life and death arose as I battled in the throes of my misery.

I thought, "God, if you are going to take me, let's not drag this out! Make it quick!" The illness stayed with me for only a few additional hours, but the duration seemed like a lifetime. *"Why me, and why now? Why me, and why now?"* became my fervently repeated mantra. Then, around 2:30 in the morning, I had a revelation! Even if God had shown up, sat down next to me, put His (or Her) hand on my shoulder, and explained, "Dan, *this* is why you, and *this* is why now," I would not have felt any better. I was asking the wrong question! I changed my prayer and my question to one much more straightforward: "What is mine to do?"

Instantly, as clearly as could be, I received an answer, a simple one. I needed to lie down and put cool, wet cloths across my chest and my forehead. After doing that, I fell asleep in minutes. I awoke refreshed, maybe a bit weak, but excited about the new lesson I was about to share with the congregation — a lesson learned by experience combined with a willingness to listen to guidance.

Now, whenever I feel anguish, disappointment, or fear and I want to know what to do, I ask a better question than "Why did this happen?" or "What kind of person would do this?" and certainly not "Why me and why now?" Rather, I ask "What is mine to do?" Guidance comes to those who are ready to receive it, who are willing to follow it, and who will simply remember to ask the right question.

Steps for Deeper Understanding

Consider a challenge or problem you face. Rather than asking victim questions, which really have no answer, ask yourself "What is mine to do?"

Decide to take the first step toward answering that question for yourself.

Notice how you feel as you follow your inner guidance.

Notes:_____

_____

_____

_____

DAY 25: COINCIDENCE?

There's a lot more going on than just what we see with our eyes. Events and circumstances may come together in the most unanticipated ways. Everyone has experienced a synchronicity that cannot be explained with logic. Is it a coincidence that you are reading this page? Is there even really such a thing as coincidence?

I have heard so many stories from people about the amazing "chance occurrences" that have happened in their lives. Out of nowhere, the right help shows up. Out of nowhere, the person they were just thinking of, whom they have not thought of for years, calls them. People meet, by chance, and find they have the most unusual connections or interest in common. (Interestingly, as I was writing this article, someone dropped by my office to share an amazing coincidence that just happened in her life!)

While I do not believe our lives are predestined, I do believe that often much more goes on than meets the eye when serendipitous events happen. I also believe, with a person's willing awareness, these events can be identified more frequently. While a person *could* constantly try to read every possible connection into every event, doing so would probably be a waste of time. However, we can become attuned to a perceptible spiritual connection. We can discern which circumstance has specific meaning for us and then glean the guidance that helps us decide what to do with the information we receive.

For example, you may be seeking a job, and an employer may be seeking a worker with a specific set of talents and characteristics you happen to possess. You are both exhibiting hopeful and expectant energy. Then, somehow, you find each other — not merely meeting at an interview, but in such a way that at that meeting, you both have a feeling of mutuality about the connection. I have had that feeling, both as a job seeker and as an employer. For many people, sometimes unlikely and even extraordinary circumstances have resulted in a perfect matchup with a "chance" connection.

What does coincidence have to do with you and me? What does coincidence have to do with living a spiritual life? We cannot disconnect our spiritual life from any other aspect of life. We can ignore it, we can doubt it, we can even challenge it, but our spiritual life will be there always. Wouldn't it be more helpful to acknowledge this aspect of life and reap the benefits of awareness? Being mindful, conscious, and "in the moment" never hurts us. The universe is constantly giving us "hints." An energy, an ever-present guidance, seeks to express to us as a route to our highest good.

You can tap into that energy, that guidance. But how do you know if your guidance is from God? I once received this explanation: When the orchestra is warming up before a concert, all you hear is the cacophony of instrumentation, all playing at once, no tune, no melody, just noise. Suddenly, even though the conductor has already been standing there for a while, all the noise stops. The conductor has tapped a baton lightly on the music stand; somehow, every orchestra member has heard it. How? With all the noise, how have they heard that little tap-tap-tap?

They learned to listen for it! They learned to discern *that* sound from all the other sounds. In addition, they were consciously aware of the need to listen.

We can learn to discern, too. We can hear the voice of God — the still, small voice, the gentle whisper, the nudge, the inner knowing, the intuition — if we learn to discern. Notice your feelings when thinking about something or someone. Are you over-thinking? Are you mentally investigating every possible scenario? Are you reacting versus responding to a situation?

Sometimes, our guidance comes to us in a dream, or as an "aha!" Spiritual Guidance may show up as coincidence, especially if that coincidence is repeated. This shared guidance is to our benefit. What Spirit wants for us is always in our highest interest. Our job is to be aware, to live in the now moment, and to listen for our own little tap-tap-tap.

Steps for Deeper Understanding

What is the last coincidence you can remember happening to you?

Did this coincidence have special meaning or trigger certain feelings or memories?

Today, choose to "learn to discern" the voice and way of Spirit through the synchronicities you observe.

Notes:_____

_____

_____

_____

DAY 26: BEYOND APPEARANCES

Appearances can be deceiving. We rarely know what we are looking at, really. You (a customer) see a clerk at the grocery store; that clerk sees a customer (you). Yet both persons are so much more. We each have multiple pieces to our personalities and past experiences. Some of us are mothers or fathers, sisters or brothers. Some folks were business owners, some were nurses, others work outside or from a home office with their computers. Each of us has a story. Each of us is both a teacher and a student, if we let ourselves be.

But we tend to limit others and ourselves by putting people in categories. We do this almost instantly, as a learned habit. We notice their clothes, the hair (or lack of it), the cars they drive, even the groceries they buy. We also compare. People are either thinner or larger than we are. They speak a different language than ours, their skin is a different color than ours, they sound like they come from the Northeast, or Deep South, or perhaps a foreign country. Using our five senses to understand the world is normal. But all religions agree that life is more than what we cognitively comprehend. We are called to use our faith to experience what is invisible.

Jesus was able to see beyond physical appearances to the spiritual. He not only demonstrated his divinity but also called people higher at the same time. Often in the Scriptures, when someone desired to be healed of their afflictions, Jesus asked if they believed they could be healed. When they answered in the affirmative, he often would comment that their faith had made them well. Jesus saw that they, and we, have an innate power to heal ourselves. If we combine the power of faith with our imagination, we can envision a healing and open ourselves to that healing. I have seen this happen many times. When people who were feeling overcome with grief and fear chose to see differently, to feel and imagine wholeness, "miracles" occurred.

Unity students understand the stories, places and people of the Bible metaphysically. In other words, Unity ascertains a higher truth than just the literal story. The Bible stories are *our* stories. David, for instance, was a shepherd boy who decided to take on the giant Philistine, Goliath. Goliath wore several pieces of heavy armor; David's supporters outfitted him similarly. But hardly able to move under the weight, David shed his armor and fought Goliath with the one tool he knew, the sling he used to keep wild animals from the sheep. Of course, David killed the giant with one stone to the forehead.

We understand that story is about the giant difficulties we face from time to time. These problems — such as relationship issues, financial difficulties, or health challenges — may freeze us in fear, in helplessness, or in other ways and keep us from facing them. It may be a relationship problem, or a financial difficulty, or a health challenge. We believe that with prayer, meditation, discernment, and an openness to guidance, we receive what we need to defeat our problems.

We already have the tools. Experiences we have lived through may remind us that we have the courage and the ability to face and overcome whatever we need to. We are guided to the right doctor or procedure, for instance. Or we receive a divine idea to help us through a financial plight. When we open our minds and hearts and check in with our intuitive knowing, our fear and anxiety diminish.

We need to know that spiritual principles *always* work. That's not a secret: spiritual principles live in every religion. Author Jeffrey Moses wrote *Oneness*, which compared the major religions. Amazingly, they mostly teach the same basic truths: Love your neighbor. Do to others as you would have them do to you. Love your enemies.

If we would see with spiritual eyes and hear with spiritual ears, we would not get so caught up in the everyday craziness of life. Rather, we would see beyond appearances to the good that God would have us see. We deserve to experience our good, to know the higher truth that is based on faith. The next time we find ourselves crying that the sky is falling, let us stop, take a moment to breathe, and know that there is always a greater understanding — and that we already have the tools to see beyond appearances.

Steps for Deeper Understanding

Notice the inclination to place judgments on others or yourself. If you become judgmental, stop for just a moment and take a deep breath.

Take a few more seconds today to notice other people and to notice your circumstances. Do so simply, with a sense of curiosity.

Remember that we are all spiritual beings having a human experience.

Notes:_____

_____

_____

_____

DAY 27: PRAYING THE PERFECT PRAYER

One of my favorite scriptures is Mark 11:24 (NRSV): "So I tell you, whatever you ask for in prayer, believe that you have received it, and it will be yours." Let me tell you why.

This scripture says it all. It incorporates the four dimensions of being: spiritual, mental, emotional, and physical.

Of course, praying is a spiritual activity, one based in faith. The "pray-er" believes, at some level, that prayer goes beyond oneself; that prayer is "heard" or known by God, Spirit, the Universe; and that prayer may receive a response.

Mentally, one puts into words a prayer, whether out of desperation or worry or fear, or from a place of gratitude or peace or hope. Many people have learned specific prayers since childhood — prayers before dinner, at bedtime, in church. Whatever brings to a person a feeling of connection with something greater is a substantive prayer.

Emotion activates prayer energy. Feeling a prayer is not only achievable but can even be answered to our greatest expectation is an expression of faith. The Scripture says to believe we have already received what we are asking for, and it will be ours. The limitation is in our ability to believe fully. I wonder, though, if Jesus didn't also add, "This, or something even better" at the end of his prayers. So often, we receive answered prayer in ways that surpass our small thinking — answers that, in time, we see were even greater than what we hoped for or expected.

I have found that the emotional state we are praying *from* is much more important than what we are praying *for*. Prayer is a form of energy. A great law of the universe is that we draw to ourselves that to which we give energy. If we pray from a place of anxiety or distress, we tend to dwell on and experience those things. If, however, we can take even a moment in absolute faith and feel a sense of peace, relief, or simply willingness, we move from the high-stress emotional state and become more able to see and accept answered prayer.

The physical dimension is where reality lives. Acting as if my prayer is answered means that if I pray for a job, I don't look longingly at the telephone or emails for hours each day, waiting for my answer. I get up, go out, and do whatever I think I need to do in order to be fully ready for answered prayer. I pick out the clothes I will wear at work, I learn all about the company or industry I want to work in, I imagine the perfect interview, and I may even do some volunteer work in a related field. If I am praying for a new home, I go to open houses to get clear on exactly what I want, I shop for the right mortgage company, and I get pre-qualified. These are practical ways for "putting feet on our prayers."

Let us notice where we are putting our mental, emotional, physical, and spiritual energy. Regardless of the words, or lack of them, we may be praying more than we think we are! The opportunity is to be clear, be willing, and believe. Truthfully, any prayer that connects us more profoundly to the Divine is the right and perfect prayer.

Steps for Deeper Understanding

When you pray, intentionally, what thoughts and feelings accompany your prayer?

Place special attention on the energy from which you are praying. Is it fearful? Curious? Expectant?

Imagine yourself receiving exactly what you prayed for. What are the accompanying feelings? Hold onto them — that IS the prayer!

Notes:_____

_____

_____

_____

ACTION

Regardless of our awareness and our attitude, we cannot truly take charge of our life if we do not take some form of action. This requires faith, willingness, and courage. We are spurred on by our ability to imagine the best and go for it. We don't always know exactly what step to take at any given time, but we can rest assured that if we don't take a step we will stay exactly where we are. It may feel a bit scary to step out of our known and comfortable way of being. We are, however, here at this time on purpose. We are here to be all we are created to be. Life requires taking risks if we are to grow our soul - and that is exactly what we are here to do!

FAITH/IMAGINATION

Faith is Spiritualized Imagination.

— *Henry Ward Beecher*

We all have a power of faith, and we use it all the time. The challenge we sometimes face, though, is *how* we use it. We may have practiced a pessimistic faith, constantly finding evidence that things just are not working out well for us. *As we believe, so it is for us.*

The good news is that just by noticing that things are difficult, just by our conscious awareness of our upset, concern, or misery, we have the beginning of a solution. We have been given the power of choice. We can change our thoughts. We, and we alone, are in charge of our attitude. Moreover, we do not have to hit bottom before moving back up to where we need to be. Faith is the invisible power with visible results.

DAY 28: ACTION CURES FEAR

Action cures fear. A friend of mine said that once in a Sunday sermon, and I realized immediately the power of those three words. Doing something — making a call, taking the time to follow up on a worrisome situation, making a commitment and following through on it — eliminated or lessened the fear.

Fear is generally much worse than the thing which is feared itself. Much of what I have feared in life has come not from my reality, but from my imagination. I have worried or fretted about circumstances I envisioned, using the "worst case scenario." I'm not alone. The other day, my wife got into the passenger side of the car, and, as we were driving away, she looked up, and screamed. Since her frightened screaming does not make for comfortable driving, I stopped right away. Kathy pointed to a large spider just inches from her face. Luckily, the arachnid was on the outside of the window, a fact not immediately apparent. The spider was real, as was the fear, even though the threat was not.

We make up (or buy into) our fears. I am told that we are born with only two fears, falling and loud noises; the rest are learned. Certainly some fears are appropriate and healthy, such as the fear instilled in us about running out into traffic. Most fears, however, keep us from living more peaceful and happy lives.

While much less prevalent today, at one time many people feared flying. Actually, the fear was more likely of falling than flying, but all the air safety statistics will do little to allay a deeply indwelling fear. However, actually taking one flight, and then another, and then another gradually dissipates the fear of flying. The same is true for just about any fear.

The experience of overcoming a fear can be one of our greatest transformational moments, freeing and actually strengthening us. We move ever more fearlessly through life.

In Luke 12:22-23 (NRSV), Jesus reminded his disciples, "Therefore I tell you, do not worry about your life, what you will eat, or about your body, what you will wear. For life is more than food, and the body more than clothing." Jesus, who called not only the brave, but also the willing, tells us not to worry.

Humans have developed many fears over time: fear of commitment, change, rejection, the unknown, death, failure, forgetting, pain, punishment, poverty, public speaking, and even fear of being wrong. Susan Jeffers, author of *Feel the Fear and Do It Anyway* maintains: "Pushing through fear is less frightening than living with the bigger underlying fear that comes from a feeling of helplessness!"

We deserve to live life above and beyond our fears. As that terror rises from time to time from the pits of our stomachs, let's just stop, breathe, and ask ourselves, "Is this real, or am I filling myself with negative 'what if's'? What can I do to push through this fear?"

As you confront your fears, as you take a calm and thoughtful moment to inspect the reality, and as you make a conscious choice to respond to your situation rather than react, you will find that your consciousness, your inner will, and your faith are bigger than any imagined worry. You do not have to obey the fight or flight response. You do not need to live in dread, anxiety, panic, or trepidation. You *can* push through. Action cures fear!

Steps for Deeper Understanding

Think about a time in the past you may have misused your imagination to make something more fearful than it really was.

Reflect more deeply. What is the earliest you can remember having this (or a similar) fear? What do you think has caused this fear?

Identify a situation/circumstance in your life today that is causing anxiety or fear. Consider one small action step you could take this week that would help you overcome or at least confront that fear. For instance, if you fear public speaking, speak up in a group this week.

Notes:_____

_____

_____

_____

DAY 29: THE "F" WORD

Growing up, I was afraid of the "F" word. Not until my mid-thirties did I become aware of the power and reality of "F"aith. Now, "faith" is an everyday practice for me. Faith is an invisible power or energy that we use all the time.

Some people have been called "persons of faith," but I don't believe they have any more faith than anyone else, just as I don't believe one person is closer to God than another is. The difference may be how focused we are as we use our faith.

We may get confused by the use of the word "faith." While faith certainly can have a spiritual context, it is also simply part of the way we think. We have faith that the sun will come up tomorrow, but we no longer pray and make sacrifices to the Sun God. We have faith that someone will pick up the trash each week. We have faith that the next breath we take will not be our last, and that is almost always true, is it not?

But faith, like any other power or energy, may be wrongly used. If we spend a great deal of our time worrying, we are using the power of faith in negative ways. Faith, like prayer, is co-creative. When we worry regularly and find that our worries and concerns are seemingly justified, we are keeping positive outcomes from our realms of possibilities by the way we think!

What if we choose a different path? What if we choose to imagine life circumstances working in beneficial ways for ourselves and for our loved ones? I believe that through our faith and beliefs, we open or close doors to the positive possibilities that life seeks to share with us. I also believe we will receive indications and signs of those possibilities along the way.

God, the Universe, the Force — whatever you may call this concept — provides evidence of a deeper knowing, a mystical "something" that seeks to guide or comfort us.

Let me share a personal example of faith in action. We once took our beloved Bernese Mountain dog Brenna to the veterinarian's office for a relatively simple procedure, teeth cleaning, a job we were not so skilled at. The doctor routinely recommended a blood test, since Brenna would be under anesthesia and certain conditions could prove dangerous if we were unaware of them.

The tests indicated Brenna had serious health problems. X-rays showed a huge growth on her liver and lung cancer that had already completely destroyed one lung. Her condition could not be improved with any sort of operation or treatment. Our only option was to keep her comfortable for as long as we could, and know, as our veterinarian told us, that "each day is a gift."

We were devastated by the news. Brenna might be with us for only days or weeks. She weakened steadily, eventually having difficulty just standing up. We decided to take her in for an evaluation, knowing that this might be her last one, a traumatic experience, as anyone who has lost a beloved pet knows.

It was time. We were with her during her last moments, loving Brenna through it all as she passed on peacefully. We had faith that this was the right thing to do and the right time to do it, yet we also experienced all that goes on at such a time of grieving.

Here's where the sign comes in, the happening we could not put down to coincidence. We had never seen another Bernese Mountain dog in our small town in the four years we had lived there. Yet as soon as we left the exam room, just feet from where Brenna had passed away, were two beautiful Bernese Mountain puppies, just a few months old. Feeling their energy and petting them, we were reminded that more is always going on in this universe than we are aware of, and that through faith and with an open mind and heart, we will always find evidence of God.

Steps for Deeper Understanding

How could I be using faith wrongly?

Do I truly believe God (the Universe, Force, and so on) wants me to have my highest and best?

I choose today to find evidence of God. (Come back to this step later to fill in the details!)

Notes:_____

_____

_____

_____

DAY 30: THERE'S NOT A DOWNSIDE TO LOOKING UP

When people say they have faith in God, I wonder what they really mean. Do they mean they believe God will intervene in life on their behalf? Or that God will do something special for them in their time of need?

Faith is a force, an energy that is often misunderstood. Faith has sometimes been related to the sacrifice a person makes in the name of God, whether by congregating with fellow believers or by living according to certain religious principles. Faith may include these things, but it is so much more.

Faith is not a matter of "let's make a deal" with the Divine, but a force that combines the power of imagination with the power of one's belief, resulting in the manifestation of circumstances, opportunities, feelings, or healings.

(Hebrews 11:1 ESV) The Bible defines faith as "the assurance of things hoped for, the conviction of things unseen" (Hebrews 11:1). In truth, we are practicing faith every day, whether we realize it or not. How so?

What do you believe about your life circumstances? Do you believe that your relationships with others are filled with great and mutual satisfaction? Do you wake up each morning believing that this may be the best day you have ever lived? Or do you go through life waiting for the other shoe to drop, for the bottom to fall out, expecting the worst and often finding exactly what you expected to find?

Henry Ford once wisely observed, "If you think you can, or if you think you can't — you're right." We have a choice to make. We are actually creating or blocking opportunities in life through our beliefs, through where and how we place our faith. How can we change that?

Could you agree that the universe is conspiring to support you? The concept is intriguing, yet I can easily point to times in my life I felt anything but supported! I've had times that felt as if everything and everyone was against me — and I had proof!

However, when I am open and honest with myself, I realize that as a victim of my circumstances, I dug into my position. I justified and even defended my victimhood! Blaming others, or circumstances, for my seeming failures or challenges was easier than facing the cold, hard fact that I, and only I, was deciding my attitude about any situation I faced.

What if I decided to view my circumstances differently? Same circumstances, different perspective. Life is really *for* me, not against me, and conditions I face are working together in positive ways, for my good. Is it possible that my belief that the world (or at least some portion thereof) was out to get me was a misuse of the power of faith?

Perhaps faith is as much a scientific endeavor as it is spiritual or religious. Perhaps we can be observers and therefore students of an experiment of applied faith.

Let's test this hypothesis. Consider a difficult situation or a challenging relationship you are facing. What thoughts and emotions arise? You may find yourself justifying your position, finding an appropriate amount of blame to aim, believing that since the problem is out of your hands, nothing you can do will heal or remedy the problem.

Believing that you are powerless is misusing faith. Whatever you believe, you empower. A simple shift in thought, and thereby also in emotion, can open doors to new possibilities. Choose to believe, if only for the sake of this experiment, that the situation not only has a solution, but that the solution contains within it a gift of some sort that will benefit you now and also in the future. Take that within for a few minutes and feel the difference. Affirmative possibility thinking is a positive use of the power of faith, uplifting, constructive, confident, and progressive.

When you combine these thoughts and feelings you are making a shift that will have a positive result. You may need to give up the exact details of the result, but you can have faith in the positivity of applied faith.

For now, take the grand experiment, prove the positive possibilities, and know for yourself you will never again be falling flat on your faith. Remember — there is not a downside to looking up!

Steps for Deeper Understanding

Go to bed tonight deciding that tomorrow will be one of the greatest days of your life.

Remind yourself upon awakening to look for proof of the above.

Take a few moments in quiet meditation to feel the energy of an absolute and undeniable blessing in your life today.

Notes:_____

_____

_____

_____

Steps for Deeper Understanding

CHANGE

You could not step twice into the same rivers, for other
waters are ever flowing on to you.

— Heraclitus

Change is inevitable. For many people, resistance to change is just as inevitable. People become adjusted to their lifestyles, and disruption brings fear and uncertainty. Making new choices about change will ease your mind and increase your energy. Give it a try!

DAY 31: BURN YOUR BRIDGES

I remember hearing when I was younger, "Never burn your bridges." This adage made sense. I didn't want to sever a relationship based on an upset, or words said in haste, or an unmet expectation one person had of another. A healing or new understanding could take place in the future.

This advice works well for relationships. Through time and the power of forgiveness, even some of the unlikeliest reconciliations can happen.

Sometimes, though, burning your bridges is wise — and scary, yes, filling you with doubt the minute you light that match. But that burn also may be the one thing that moves you forward, on purpose with your higher purpose. In an earlier chapter I mentioned once having a job I really did not like. Not only did I *not* like what I was doing, but I also felt like I was being untrue to myself. I needed to move on.

After giving my two-week notice, I had the biggest sale of my life. Of course, I re-thought my initial decision to leave. But leave I did… kind of… almost.

As I was making major changes in the type of work I was doing, I held onto all my licenses, just in case. I could still sell stocks, bonds, life/health/disability insurances, and annuities with another firm if I needed to.

The major changes I planned, however, didn't "take." My foray into a new career was a miserable failure, and, as I had suspected and semi-planned for, I was back making telephone cold calls to people who might purchase financial products from me.

I have learned since then. Sometimes, it *is* wise to burn the bridges that would otherwise allow us to recede back into a miserable comfort zone, into a place that we know all too well that reminds us of our lack of courage and confidence.

When I entered into ministry, I burned bridges behind me, not in an unfriendly fashion, but in such a way as to assure myself that I was moving forward with faith and trusting God with my life.

For the first time in a long time, I felt a real sense of freedom! Frightening as it was to start a new endeavor without a safety net, I felt a focus and strong desire to succeed, even if I didn't know exactly how that would look.

For his book *Think and Grow Rich*, author Napoleon Hill interviewed hundreds of very successful men, many of whom were introduced to him by his mentor, Andrew Carnegie. Based upon their accumulated wisdom, Hill developed a process for people to receive what they truly desire.

Here is an adapted summary of his findings, along with some supporting scripture.

(1)Fix in your mind exactly what you desire. It is not sufficient merely to say, "I want plenty of money" or "I want a new car" or "I want a healed relationship." Be as specific as you can. Be open to inner guidance.

"Your Father knows what you need before you ask." (Matthew 6:8) (Matthew 7:2 NRSV)

(2)Determine exactly what you intend to give in return for what you desire. (There is no such reality as "something for nothing.")

"For with the judgment you make you will be judged, and the measure you give will be the measure you get." (Matthew 7:2 NRSV)

(3)Establish a definite date when you intend to have what you desire. Listen to your inner guidance.

"The Lord will guide you continually. . . ." (Isaiah 58:11 NRSV)

". . . in due season we shall reap, if we do not lose heart." (Galatians 6:9 NKJV)

(4)Create a definite plan for carrying out your desire, and begin at once, whether you are ready or not, to put this plan into action.

> "I am about to do a new thing; now it springs forth,
> do you not perceive it?"

> (Isaiah 43:19 NRSV)

(5)Write out a clear, concise statement of your intention, state what you intend to give in return, name the time limit for its acquisition, and create your plan clearly.

(6)Read your written statement aloud twice daily, once just before retiring at night, and once after arising in the morning. *As you read — see and feel and believe your prayers have been answered — your desires have been fulfilled.*

> "Therefore I tell you, do not worry about your life, what you will eat or what you will drink, or about your body, what you will wear. Is not life more than food, and the body more than clothing?

> Look at the birds of the air; they neither sow nor reap nor gather into barns, and yet your heavenly Father feeds them. Are you not of more value than they?"

> (Matthew 6:25-26 NRSV)

Step out in faith. Burning bridges is not recommended for relationship building, but it may be *exactly* what you need for dream building. Dream on!

Steps for Deeper Understanding

In what area of your life are you procrastinating, not following through on a decision you know you need to make?

Imagine you have moved forward. You made the decision and acted on it. Project yourself to the other side of that. How do you feel?

Taking the chance to step out in faith is the best way to build more faith. Choose to demonstrate the courage to show yourself that you believe in you!

Notes:_____

_____

_____

_____

DAY 32: TRANSFORMATION

Spring is a time of newness, a time of transformation. Nature awakens from a long slumber as daylight increases. Even where I live in Florida, I see evidence of the season's change. Spring brings new blossoms, new baby birds and bunnies, and a new freshness in the air.

When I hear the word "transformation," I immediately think of nature. I think about a caterpillar weaving a cocoon or forming a chrysalis, and, over time, experiencing metamorphosis. The caterpillar deconstructs and then reconstructs to become a moth or a butterfly moving from the relatively simple to the relatively profound, from very limited to virtually unlimited, free to fly.

I find the transformation and beauty of the butterfly intriguing. When I was a child, I collected butterflies and moths, often catching, carefully examining, and then releasing them. Even today, my mood brightens whenever I see a butterfly or moth flitting from flower to flower or stretching its wings in the sunlight.

Another thought that comes to me with the word "transformation" has to do with the internal changes we each make as we grow through life. Through our hardships as well as our achievements, we become different people, not the same as we were before and never the same again. From those points on, even if we face similar difficulties or have similar opportunities, we face them with greater poise and confidence.

Transformation of this kind is an upward movement. A desire deep within us relates to the idea of breaking through from one way of living to another, greater way of life.

Yet we still often resist change. We do not want to release the "old us" that is so familiar with the status quo, even if that has become uncomfortable. We may suffer through our days, enduring our circumstances, unhappy, but unwilling to risk the possibility of our lives being even worse than they are.

So, we don't look for the fulfilling job. We don't "clean up" the messy or difficult relationships we have by saying what needs to be said or by forgiving or making amends. We don't listen to the creative rumble that is seeking to be fulfilled.

I have heard this uneasy feeling referred to as "divine discontent." It is the soul's way of getting our attention, not totally dissimilar to the "still, small voice" we read about in the Bible in 1 Kings 19. The awareness of God was not to be found in all the outer happenings — the strong winds, the earthquake, the fire — but rather heard as we become still and listen.

Life happens without absolute guarantees. For example, an accident or an illness or even an amazing opportunity changes life, at least for a time. Incidents happen, and we deal with them as they occur. We have the resources to handle anything that comes our way.

But what about the creative rumblings? They invite us to step up to life in a new way. They invite us into the process of transformation. Like the caterpillar, we may have to deconstruct some ways of being in order to reconstruct something new, but that is the worthwhile price of true change.

We are continually being invited into greater living. We are nudged, we are urged on, to express more of all we can be. To succeed requires spiritual awareness, faith, and courage. But we bring about transformation by listening to the still, small voice, to the divine discontent, and then taking brave action as guided. We emerge new beings, more able than ever before to live on purpose with our purpose.

Making excuses is much easier than making headway. Yet we do not want our legacy to be about just getting by. Transformation requires letting go of the safety net and moving forward at the speed of guidance. As French author Andre Gide wrote, "One doesn't discover new lands without consenting to lose sight, for a very long time, of the shore."

Steps for Deeper Understanding

Look back on the last several years and notice how you have changed for the better as you dealt with life's circumstances. Name one or two such changes that stand out for you.

While these circumstances may have been difficult for you, can you see how you have grown wiser as a result?

What creative rumblings are happening in your life today? Listen, and take positive action as guided.

Notes:_____

_____

_____

_____

DAY 33: A CHANGE OF SEASONS

When I was around 8 years old, I wrote a short poem about the seasons, which I was proud of: "Spring has sprung, and Fall has fell. Summer's here and it's hotter than — well, it's hotter than it was last year." I also remember living up north as a young man, seeing the snow melt as springtime neared, putting down the convertible top when the temperature reached about 36° F, and watching for crocuses to push through the slightly-less-than-frozen ground. Buds appeared on the trees, and the days began to stretch longer. While spring does not bring such dramatic changes here in Florida, new beginnings are still a seasonal sign. Turtle nesting season begins in March. Snowbird season ends in April or May. Hurricane season starts in June.

We are always dealing with change, even if we are trying to avoid it. Many people are quite resistant to change, though. Once our routines are set, once we find the right doctor or join the organizations that we want to support, once we are doing what we love with those we love, the last thing we want is change. But since change is going to happen, we can choose to embrace it, rather than fear it or become upset by it.

In order to handle change better, remember these three magic words: "Isn't that interesting?" We take the charge out of the various ways life comes at us by living in a place of nonresistance. We de-escalate the energy of upset by choosing to take things in stride, trusting that we will somehow always have whatever we need to deal with, whatever we must deal with. Another name for that is faith.

We can all look back on times when we had major challenges to handle. In the moment, we may have felt confused or lost. Maybe we had no idea how, when, or even if we could get through the difficulty or the chaos. But we did. Each time, we grew in faith. We had what we needed when we needed it, strength, friends or family, inspiration, or anything else.

As we move forward into this day, this week, this life, let us do so with positive expectation and nonresistance. What God (Spirit, the Force) wants for us always is our highest and best. We are much more likely to experience our good by living with a positive expectation for that good. But, once again, that is our choice.

I read recently in Brene' Brown's book *Daring Greatly* about a man who decided to live by always expecting the worst. That way, when the worst did not happen, he would feel better. If the worst did actually happen, he would be prepared. So he lived his whole life looking for what could go wrong, not fully appreciating or enjoying all that was going right. Then he had a car accident, and his wife of forty years was killed. Not only was he unprepared for such a tragedy, but, even more sadly, he had passed up so many opportunities to live his life with her in better, more enjoyable ways. He vowed to never again ignore any opportunity to live his life fully and instead to savor every moment, as his commitment to her.

Metaphorically, we are going through a change of seasons on a regular basis. Let's open to change and be thankful for change in our lives. When change happens — and it will — let us declare wholeheartedly, and with great faith, "Isn't that interesting?"

Steps for Deeper Understanding

Changes are always happening. What changes are you "putting up with" and what changes do you want to purposefully make?

Choose, for at least a short time, to see the possible good in the changes you are resisting.

Feel the sense of peace, and the faith, that nonresistance brings you.

Notes:_____

_____

_____

DAY 34: GROWING THROUGH THE CHANGES IN LIFE

Behind our church lies a Labyrinth, designed for a walking meditation. Nearby, we have a meditation bench surrounded by a beautiful butterfly garden. All the life in this ecosystem is amazing to see! The blooms of the Jacaranda tree are blue and purple. Flowers of various shapes, sizes, and colors attract butterflies, which dance from flower to flower. This meditation garden brings me a sense of immediate peace. At least for a few moments, all is well with the world.

Over time, I have watched these plants grow, which was challenging, especially at first. Getting the right amount of water at the right time required teamwork with staff and volunteers, but the effort paid off.

Growth is natural, but not necessarily easy. In order to develop, an organism must push through challenges. Of course, we have similar challenges. We face unpredictable weather. We have some storms in our lives. Yet we grow, sometimes becoming even stronger because of the storms.

Growth is like that. We encounter different circumstances, and we push through to a new and higher understanding. The struggle is often necessary, creating momentum to propel us on to new things.

What areas are tugging at you for spiritual growth? Generally, you can tell by just observing what makes you uncomfortable. Of course, discomfort isn't the only sign. If that were so, then stubbing your toe would be a sign of growth. Usually other signs appear when you are ready to take the next step. Where we feel intimidated or incomplete or fearful is exactly where we can put our attention so we can grow through or past these situations. Signs may come in the form of opportunities or challenges. Often, circumstances avail themselves to us that offer chances for a new take on life. Here it comes — another dang growth opportunity!

We have all had to make difficult decisions in life. We may have discovered that old ideas which used to work just fine no longer work. We have had to change and expand our horizons.

In truth, we are responsible for the way our lives are working or not working. Much as we might like to blame a person, an agency, heredity, or any number of other things, we, and only we, are in charge of our perceptions and actions.

Rightly comprehended, this understanding is a great blessing. We are not subject to a capricious God "out there" who punishes or rewards us based on whim. We can take charge of our own lives. We can choose to grow through anything that comes our way. We release the need to be a victim of life. We see life as a positive experience filled with opportunities for becoming all we came into this world to become. This is growth. Growth isn't easy, but it is rewarding. With God, we are co-architects of our lives. We build a life through our thoughts and actions, through prayer and meditation. We allow the goodness of God to flow through us to touch others. That's what Jesus did.

We are continually co-creating with God. As long as we are alive, we will be growing. Resisting is futile. As we grow, we can choose to find peace in the midst of struggle, and beauty and purpose in all we see.

Steps for Deeper Understanding

Think back on some of the storms in your life. How have you grown stronger spiritually?

Can you see how "mistakes" you made may have brought you much needed learning, if only to see how not to repeat them?

What will be your next "growth opportunity"?

Notes:_____

_____

_____

_____

DAY 35: NEW BEGINNINGS

The end of one year and the beginning of another offers many opportunities to make positive changes. In our church, we typically end the year with a Burning Bowl service on New Year's Eve. In this service, people consider what they would like to release, write that down on a piece of paper, and bring that paper to the Burning Bowl, tossing it in and letting it go up in flame. This ritual feels purifying: We let go of our mistakes, unwillingness to forgive, anger, unhealthy habits, regrets, and unmet expectations. We open the door (and our energy) to move into the new year unencumbered by thoughts that no longer serve a good and healthy purpose. We then write down our positive expectations of the coming year and seal that paper in a self-addressed envelope, which the church mails back to us in six months. This letter gives us amazing insight about what has transpired over that half year, as well as how much of what we envisioned for ourselves has indeed happened!

While change doesn't happen magically, a spiritual component is continually operative. We are constantly co-creating our reality by the thoughts we hold in mind. "Thoughts held in mind produce after their own kind" is a major universal spiritual principle. The thoughts we think and the feelings we feel draw to us the experiences we have in life. This realization can be exhilarating but, at the same time, somewhat daunting. If I am unhappy with circumstances in my life, am I then to blame for creating them to begin with? Certainly, we don't consciously bring painful experiences into our life on purpose. Life happens. We will have times when we face difficulties, such as health challenges, financial quandaries, or job or relationship troubles. The choice we have is how we deal with what comes our way. How long do we hold onto upset or frustration? How much energy do we put into justifying our misery, or blaming someone or something else?

The transformational opportunity is in knowing that we can change our lives for the better by remembering that nobody is in charge of our thoughts but ourselves. We can stress and fuss over everything happening in our lives; or we can stop, take a breath, and make a more positive and purposeful choice. What can we learn from our circumstances? Are we repeating behaviors over and over, yet expecting different results? Are we putting all our attention on our difficulties and ignoring that which is working well in our lives? A simple shift in our attention can make all the difference in the world. Stepping back from our problems for even a short time can not only provide a new perspective, but also help us find answers when we feel helpless.

We can choose to release the burdens of negative thinking we have been carrying for far too long. Life offers us much to be positive about, and good already fills our lives. I believe we are constantly being guided and supported in ways we often cannot see. Jesus said, "It is your Father's good pleasure to give you the kingdom." (Luke 12:32) Accepting that gift as we let go and let God be God in our lives is up to us.

Steps for Deeper Understanding

Try a burning bowl experiment. Write down on a piece of paper what you are ready to release, and then burn (or shred or rip) it up.

Write down your positive expectations for the next six months and store the paper where you can easily find it again. Set a calendar reminder to open and review that list on a specific date to see how you did!

Each night, take a moment to let go of any resentments built up during that day. Feel the lightness in your soul.

Notes:_____

_____

_____

DAY 36: WE ARE MAKING PROGRESS!

I think I want the affirmation "I am making progress" as my epitaph. Yes, we are making progress. Sometimes, though, we may appear to be taking two steps backward for each step forward.

So much has to do with attitude. I need to remind myself that I make progress with my "mistakes" as well as my successes, if I choose to learn from them. I need only persevere.

We have all had regrets: things we did or did not do or say and opportunities we let pass us by. While we can acknowledge these regrets, giving them energy makes no sense in today's world. We have too much else to do besides looking backward all the time.

But if we feel we need to look back, let us do that from a broader, more experienced perspective. From there, we can see the bigger picture. We can let go of unrealistic expectations of ourselves or others. We obviously still have much to accomplish because we are still here, after all.

In the Unity church, we are always seeking to know more about God, about ourselves and each other, and about life. We consider ourselves to be Truth Students. Steven Covey wrote *The 7 Habits of Highly Effective People*. I can distinguish seven practices of highly effective Truth Students: Awareness, Willingness, Forgiveness, Faith, Imagination, Realization, and Practical Application.

Awareness allows us to be in the moment, neither living in the past, nor living in the future. Awareness is not about regrets or about fear of what may happen. We simply live in the present moment, with our attention and antennae up. We cannot appreciate what we do not see, nor can we change what we do not notice.

Willingness opens the door for new experiences and new ways to perceive life with an open mind. Willingness requires that we notice our resistance and our insistence to have things a certain way.

Forgiveness may be difficult for some of us, especially if we have imprinted our story of victimhood deeply in our conscious and subconscious mind. Yet one of the major teachings of almost all religions is the power of forgiveness. Forgiveness is never about letting someone "off the hook" for what they did or did not do. Rather, it is releasing the need to blame or the need to be right. Forgiveness is letting go of an energy that binds us to events of the past. We forgive as a gift to ourselves. We have better ways to spend our life energy than holding onto a lifetime of resentment.

Faith helps all that to happen. We believe our lives have an ever-present spiritual component. We read in Hebrews 11:1, "Faith is the assurance of things hoped for, the conviction of things unseen." Actually, having faith is never the problem. The challenge becomes where we place our faith. If we persist in believing that the world is miserable and all we see is evidence of how difficult life is, we will continue to experience life that way, in *negative faith*. On the other hand, *positive faith* believes in a higher order in life from which we can choose to see more optimistically. When we look for the positive, or what some may call the "blessings" in life, we will find them. Even more, though, we set up an energy, a habit, of being able to see the good and actually draw more good to ourselves.

Practicing the power of imagination, combined with the power of faith, brings our prayers into manifestation. We are able to use our imagination to see our ideal future in our mind's eye and accept that future in the present moment. Do you want a new car? Imagine that car in your driveway, all shiny and new. Imagine it is paid for or at least very affordable for you. Open your mind to listen to the divine guidance that helps you find the right and perfect way to make that happen. I have a friend who did not have the money but had the faith and imagination to manifest the white Toyota Prius she had wanted for so long. She held to her faith, and conditions all came together for her prayer to become reality.

Realization is the sixth Unity practice. We take the first five practices and choose to make them real and manifest in our lives. We must be on purpose with our purpose. We each have a reason for being. Realizing and accepting this reason is part of our job in this lifetime.

The final Unity practice is the practical application of the practices. All the high and mighty thinking we can conjure up won't necessarily become real in a regular and measurable way unless we apply the truths we learn in our everyday lives. We must be consistent. If our activity is hit or miss, our results are hit or miss. Persevere, apply the practices of a Truth Student (a student of life), and you will be able to affirm, "I am making progress!"

Steps for Deeper Understanding

From a place of awareness and willingness, choose someone or something to forgive.

Look for the best in someone or something today and write it down.

Imagine a positive possibility for yourself today, and as you do, affirm "I am making progress!"

Notes:_____

_____

_____

_____

CHOICE

Attitude is a choice. Happiness is a choice. Optimism is a choice. Kindness is a choice. Giving is a choice. Respect is a choice. Whatever choice you make makes you. Choose wisely.

— *Roy T. Bennett*

Have you ever been frozen between two possible outcomes that depend on the choice you make? We may see choice as a blessing and a curse: a blessing because we have been given the gift of free will, and a curse because our decisions have consequences. We point ourselves in the direction we think is best, and then life happens. However, we can always make a new decision when one is needed. Choose wisely!

DAY 37: IT'S YOUR CHOICE

Disaster, war, politics, disaster, storms, fires, politics, disaster, puppies.

That about sums up the evening news. Somehow, ending with something cute offsets all the horrible information broadcasters believe we want or need to hear and see. The more we deaden our senses to the challenges in our world, the less real they become to us. Paradoxically, bringing us live coverage of a person's or a country's plight tugs at our emotions yet causes us to grow callous at the same time.

"Ain't-it-awful" comments do not change the world for the better. Change requires us to live from a place of greater compassion and understanding. We can change the world, but we must begin at home, where we are, in our own bodies and our own thoughts.

Nutritionists say you are what you eat. So maybe some days you are more refried beans than spinach! Overall, what we eat either strengthens us, just maintains us, or weakens us. The dress-for-success folks say you are what you wear. Some days I'm a biker and some days a banker. In truth, we are a combination of many facets: what we do, how we feel, the beliefs we hold, our genetic makeup, and more.

Sometimes we are a long way from home. We are far from being clear on who and what we really are. We may take a personality test, a Keirsey temperament sorter, an IQ or EQ (emotional quotient) test, or simply rely on the ultimate wisdom of our astrology chart.

Defining ourselves, however, is much less vital than *discovering* ourselves. We discover who we are in life through trial and error. Unfortunately, we may face some tough times in the discovery process. We may encounter difficult relationships, or we may have to overcome physical or emotional hurdles.

Ultimately, however, as we grow and develop, our challenges often become our greatest blessings. We find that we have the strength and faith to work through our troubles and become better people because of the challenges we overcame.

We are here to discover, discern, and live our true purpose. In order for that to happen, we must allow for transformation to happen, for a deep, meaningful change to occur.

We may change the outer, only to realize that circumstances just replay themselves. I knew a man who married three times, and each time the marriage ended in a messy divorce. He was looking for the right woman; but since he was unwilling to change himself, the same results played out again and again.

Consider another example: A man named Jack became stranded on a desert island for sixteen years. A ship finally spotted the island and sent a landing party to investigate.

Jack was thrilled to be able to leave but insisted on showing the captain what he had created over time: a small home with a porch, a sitting area, a bedroom, and the best comforts he could make out of the trees and rocks the island provided.

Jack then walked the captain up a path and showed him a church he had built, complete with an altar, a seating area, inspirational paintings, and even beeswax candles.

On their way to the ship, the captain saw another path and another structure.

"What's that building?" he asked.

"Oh, that?" Jack answered. "It's the church I used to go to."

We can change outer conditions, but outer change may not be lasting. True transformation comes from inner change, which itself comes from spiritual awareness. As hard as it may be for some of us to believe, we each have an inner perfection. The more of that perfection we can discover, discern, and display, the less we will have to repeat circumstances in our lives.

Let us discover, discern, and live our true purpose. We aren't really all that far away from home. We can change the world, but we must begin where we are.

Steps for Deeper Understanding

What are some of the words you would use to describe yourself? Write them down.

Does your description feel uplifting and freeing, limiting, or something in between?

Describe how some of your more difficult times have strengthened you and provided you with fuller understanding of yourself and of life.

Notes:_____

_____

_____

_____

DAY 38: A FREE SPIRIT

I have counseled people who spent years in jobs they hated, or in relationships that were completely unfulfilling. When I asked why they stayed, they often explained that the job or relationship was something they knew. They were afraid to leave and take a chance. Life might be even worse if they did.

From the highest perspective, their gloom was the perfect opportunity for a new awareness. They could continue to make excuses for living in misery, or they could make the difficult choice to face the emerging truth: An inner drive to express who they really were through their work, their relationships, and their lives could not be denied.

I am a free spirit, as are you. We all are, really, but we often feel constrained by circumstances we believe are out of our control. The truth is that control is not the issue. We need to trust the inner guidance, the pull toward something greater that we can feel when we get quiet. Our individual spirit is always seeking to express in ways that help us grow. But that may require taking a risk, leaving a comfort zone.

We can become so comfortable in our routines that change of any kind stirs up anxiety, concern, or even fear. But the only way to grow is to move through and beyond these false prisons in which we incarcerate ourselves, to be who we came here to be.

Our goal in life certainly is not to become deaf to the gentle whisper, the inner calling, the "still, small voice" of spirit. Convenient as it may be, our goal is not to live in casual indifference to the point that we become accustomed to mediocrity. The free spirit in us *wants to and can express* in creative, energetic, fulfilling ways.

We in the United States are reminded in our Declaration of Independence that we are endowed with certain unalienable rights, according to our Founding Fathers, among them life, liberty, and the pursuit of happiness. How are we using these rights, these privileges, these sacred gifts?

Life. As we read these words, we are no doubt breathing in and out. We may be having breakfast, drinking our coffee, or sitting on the porch or behind a desk. We are alive. We have been gifted with an ability to use this bodily vehicle we currently inhabit to accomplish certain tasks here. Because we also have liberty, we can choose how we spend our precious moments. Although the happiness part is not guaranteed, the pursuit of it clearly is — if we simply make that choice.

Why wouldn't we? Yes, living life a bit more fully does require awareness plus a willingness on our part to be living on purpose, not merely accidentally. What are you being called to do that will make a positive difference? Life holds more to do than just take up space.

Beyond life, liberty, and the pursuit of happiness, you have also been endowed with uniqueness. No other person is like you. Take a chance today to stretch a bit, to listen more deeply, to honor the sacred trust the divine has in you. *Who you are* blesses the world, as you choose to express your free spirit.

Steps for Deeper Understanding

In what areas of life do you feel constrained?

If you could make changes that were guaranteed to succeed, where would you start?

What is your spirit whispering to you to be or to do? Is it time to step out in faith and make a change?

Notes:_____

_____

_____

_____

DAY 39: BREAKING MURPHY'S LAW

"If you can't say something nice, don't say anything at all!" That admonition kept us kids quiet in the Holloway household when we were having disagreements. Sometimes people say, do, and perhaps especially act in ways that can preclude kind words — and sometimes it's even harder to say nothing at all.

Words can empower and uplift as well as diminish and drag down people. An even deeper truth is that our words, thoughts, prayers, and actions can develop a set of beliefs that either empower and uplift or diminish and drag *ourselves* down.

Interestingly, whether we look for the best in a situation or for the worst in a situation, we're still bound to find it. Subtle though it may be, a habit of giving energy to the negative things in life opens the door for continued negative expectations and results to occur.

Have you ever met someone who believed the world was just against them? It seems they have the worst luck ever. And they find ways to blame others, their poor circumstances, or life itself for all the difficulties they face. They easily find evidence of their peril. They receive the smallest portion when ordering at a restaurant. They are judged by others for their (fill in the blank – size, accent, clothes, car, gender, etc.) so how could they ever succeed? They get passed over for promotions, or believe they don't get the praise they deserve.

These folks really do not take responsibility for their lives, nor do they look for the positives. As a result, they tend to see life from a dismal view that they can prove, over and over.

Consistent negative thinking causes physically debilitating results. A preponderance of thoughts, positive or negative, has definite and sometimes determinable results.

Most people have heard of Murphy's Law. In its most basic form, this "law" states, "If anything can go wrong, it will."

We may assert that rain will certainly fall because we just washed the car. We may claim that the undeserving always get the good parking spots. Even Herbert Hoover fell into this line of thinking, at least for a moment, when he declared, "About the time we think we can make ends meet, somebody moves the ends."

We can spend our lives being right about what's wrong, or we can make a bold change and look for what's right and good and whole in our lives.

Each of us has reasons to celebrate so much in life: a caring relationship, a basically healthy body, a roof over our heads and food to enjoy. We can break Murphy's Law by stopping ourselves from always looking for the problems and instead noticing the simple joys in life, the goals met, the challenges overcome.

I have a friend who often affirms, "I am the luckiest man in the world!" He has had his share of difficulties, yet they are temporary and do not depress him. Yes, he often finds himself in very positive circumstances serendipitously.

Maybe the best place to start making changes is to consider what we are grateful for. Gratitude repositions our focus and produces immediate positive results. In all likelihood, by practicing gratitude, we will also find something nice to say.

Steps for Deeper Understanding

Do you find yourself speaking negatively when the weather or other factors suddenly cause you to change your plans?

Name three things in your life today that you truly treasure and appreciate. Notice how that makes you feel.

Develop an affirmation for yourself that brings you a sense of oneness with your higher power.

Notes:_____

_____

_____

_____

DAY 40: BUTTON-FREE LIVING

Occasionally, someone hits one of my buttons. You may have had a similar experience: Someone pushes in front of you in line at the store or says something you consider rude or uncaring. We often react, rather than respond. These "So's-Your-Mama!" moments come from anger, fear, impatience, or frustration. They do not demonstrate our best behavior.

Even Jesus lost his temper from time to time. He went into the temple and overturned the tables being used by the moneychangers, saying, "It is written, 'My house shall be called a house of prayer;' but you are making it a den of robbers." (Matthew 21:13, NRSV) Jesus also called out the Pharisees and the lawyers (Luke 11:37-53) for their hypocrisy.

We all have our moments, times when buttons get pushed. However, we are born with just one button, an "innie" or an "outie." The rest of our buttons are learned. They come from our expectations of what people "should" do or say in a given circumstance. These buttons — such as blame, shame, or guilt (made famous by religion, by the way) — may have been taught to us. Perhaps our buttons come from an early belief that something about us was defective. We may have been trained to believe we were worthless, less than what we "should" be, or even stupid, and we took the message to heart.

Unfortunately, such a message can go from being a false statement about us from a thoughtless parent or sibling to a reality in our lives, based on our error belief. We may inadvertently support the message by believing that these words of others have more power than we do in our own life development.

Someone calling you stupid or ugly does not make it so. Brothers and sisters will have their moments, and some people will say things to provoke others, but at any point we can wake up. We can realize that these words, even if said with ill intent, are not who we are. In fact, such words are more likely a reflection of the speaker's own insecurities.

As we become adults, we have more options. We can continue to easily allow our feelings to get hurt, or we can heal whatever hurt has caused the button to be "push-able" to begin with. We may allow ourselves to be manipulated as children, but we can surely let that behavior go as adults.

Do you know how an elephant is trained? A baby elephant is tied to a strong rope, one it cannot break, and learns it cannot break ropes. As the elephant gets bigger, the rope can get smaller, because the elephant believes the rope is stronger than it is. Similarly, flea-circus fleas were trained in lidded jars. After hitting the tops a few times while attempting to escape, the fleas no longer jumped that high, even when the lid was removed. They had learned their limitations.

We are neither elephants nor fleas. Why do we go on believing in our false limitations, those ropes and lids that have kept us tied to old thinking that confines us to a false belief?

The goal for many people I've spoken with is to live a spiritually-based, peaceful, joy-filled life with a sense of purpose and direction. This goal requires forgiveness and a willingness to release expectations of others.

We can take steps to reduce or eliminate the buttons we've worn for so long. The first is to notice when we are reacting rather than thoughtfully responding. We can't change a behavior without first noticing it. Secondly, we can accept that we are reacting, but also accept that this is not the whole story. By reacting, we are giving power to the trigger, the button of frustration, impatience, or anger. We are choosing to be victims, based on a false belief about who we are. The third step is to remember our personal power, the capability to overcome these buttons or triggers, as well as our strength and wisdom to implement this power.

The next time you get one of your buttons pushed, breathe. Count to ten, breathe deeply, and connect to your heart-centered truth. Notice that you are at a choice point and choose to respond thoughtfully rather than react. With practice, you can reduce or even eliminate the buttons that others have pushed for so long. You can finally live Button-Free!

Steps for Deeper Understanding

Have you had your buttons pushed lately? Great! Recognize this as an opportunity to find a greater truth. Sit with it and discover the misperception so the button is removed and not just managed.

What buttons do you recognize? Can you see how and by whom they regularly get pushed? That is one key to disengaging them.

When we are full of spirit and energy, our buttons are few. As we become tired or have less energy, our buttons can become many. Awareness is vital. Take time to be still and know.

Notes:_____

_____

_____

_____

Steps for Deeper Understanding

CONCLUSION

We all have the opportunity to know God, by whatever name familiar to us. Nearly every religion would not argue with the essence of this book. We share common values, even if we do not always express them in common ways. All religions speak of the importance of love. They all share the value of faith. All religions call on all individuals to express strength and courage as they demonstrate their highest principles to the best of their ability.

Our lives will always hold times of happiness, as well as of chaos or uncertainty. My highest prayer is that we can find ways to deal with all these times by expressing our divinity, our essence. We can choose to see the value in all people and in all life. I believe we should. And I believe this is God's will.

Printed in the United States
By Bookmasters